© 2019 by Kate Anderson Foley, Ph.D., and Jenifer Anderson-Smith all rights reserved
Printed in China

This book is dedicated to our family and friends who believed
in our quest for adding our voices to the narrative.
We want children to be engaged citizens, but more than that,
we want to teach children how to be advocates
for a just and loving world.

Note to Parents

This is the story of a little girl named Ida who encounters a number of unsettling situations that cause a variety of emotions. She encounters prejudice, discrimination, and hate towards her friends and family and she is trying to make sense of it all. But with the help of her family and her sidekick owl named Smalls, Ida finds the words to express her feelings. Ida speaks out for love, tolerance, and inclusion of all people, cultures, beliefs, and faiths.

There is an Ida in each one of us! All it takes is one kind action or one kind word and the belief that every person deserves dignity and acceptance in order to make our world more just, loving, and tolerant.

As a parent, it can sometimes be hard to find just the right words to help your child make sense of prejudice and intolerance, but you're just the right person! Find the Ida in you and don't be afraid to **start the conversation.** You will find other parents who want to join the conversation, and who knows, you might just start something extraordinary!

Here are some tools you can use right now to start the conversation.

- Visit your local library for books or events on these topics. Learning together fosters resiliency.

- Explore cultural events in person or virtually to learn about the many wonderful ways people live and celebrate. This empowers children with the knowledge and acceptance of people who are different than them.

Ida woke up as she did every other day ~ *a happy and kind girl* who liked to play outside, ride her bike, and have fun adventures with her mom and dad. Ida also liked learning new things at school, especially math and science. Mondays were her favorite because it was Show and Share day.

On this particular Monday, Ida was going to bring her favorite stuffed animal, an *owl named Smalls*, to show and share all about her fun trip to the science center's owl exhibit.

Ida liked owls because they came in all *different sizes, shapes, and colors.*

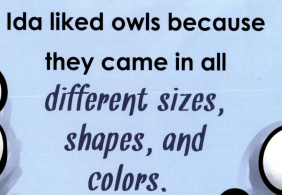

She also really liked how their heads turned all the way around to see everything. She thought that's what made owls *wise.*

After breakfast, Ida skipped to the bus, hopped on, and found her favorite seat. The next stop was her friend Dev. Ida liked listening to Dev tell about all the fun places he went with his family over the weekend.

But on this particular day, Ida heard something that made her get a *strange* feeling in her stomach, but she didn't have the words to explain how she felt.

You see, Dev got on and off the bus in a different way because he wore braces on his legs and climbing stairs was hard for him. So just like every other morning, Ms. Jones lowered the lift so Dev could get on and then raised it until it reached the floor of the bus. Once on the bus, Dev made his way to his seat next to Ida. That's when Ida heard two boys making fun of the way Dev walked.

Ida thought, "*Ouch!* Don't they know Dev's braces help him walk?" She looked at Dev who heard it too, and they both got quiet.

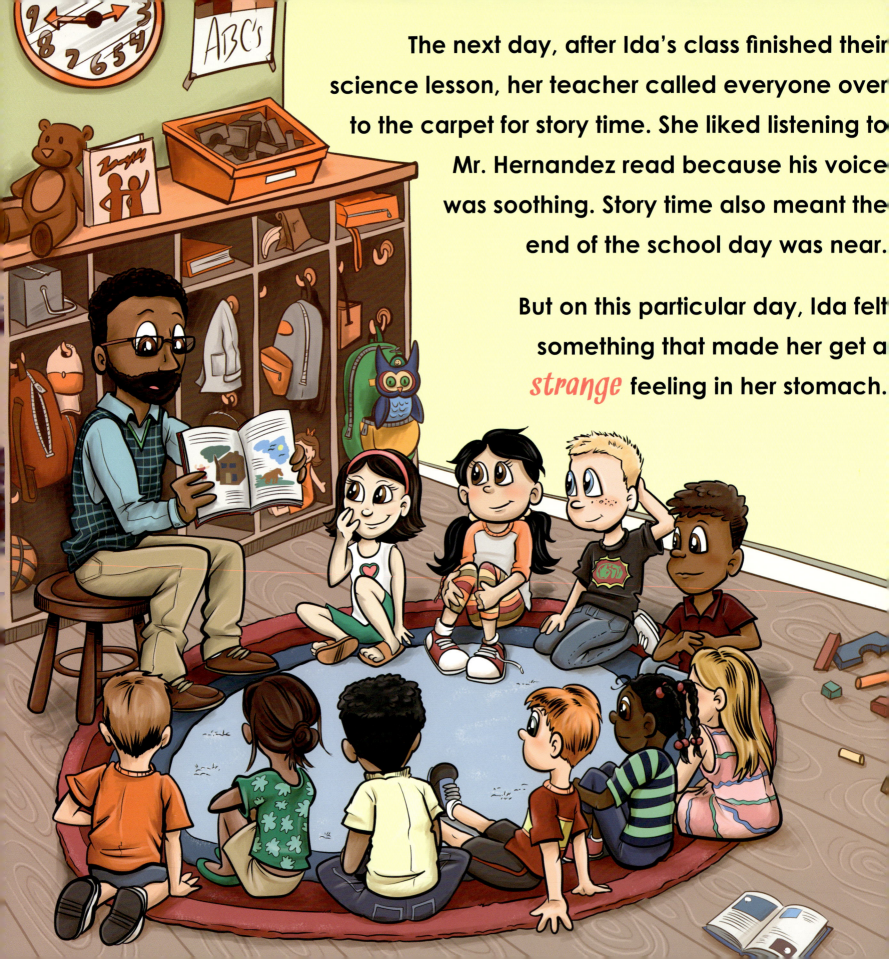

Ida had found a cozy spot on the carpet when a boy named Tommy sat down way too close to her. He hugged Ida but she didn't want to be hugged. Ida didn't want to be mean to Tommy, but she just didn't want to be touched.

I know WHO will bring the hero out in YOU.

She wanted to tell Tommy she didn't want to be hugged but she didn't have the right words. Ida thought, "Doesn't Tommy know he shouldn't touch someone unless they say it's okay?"

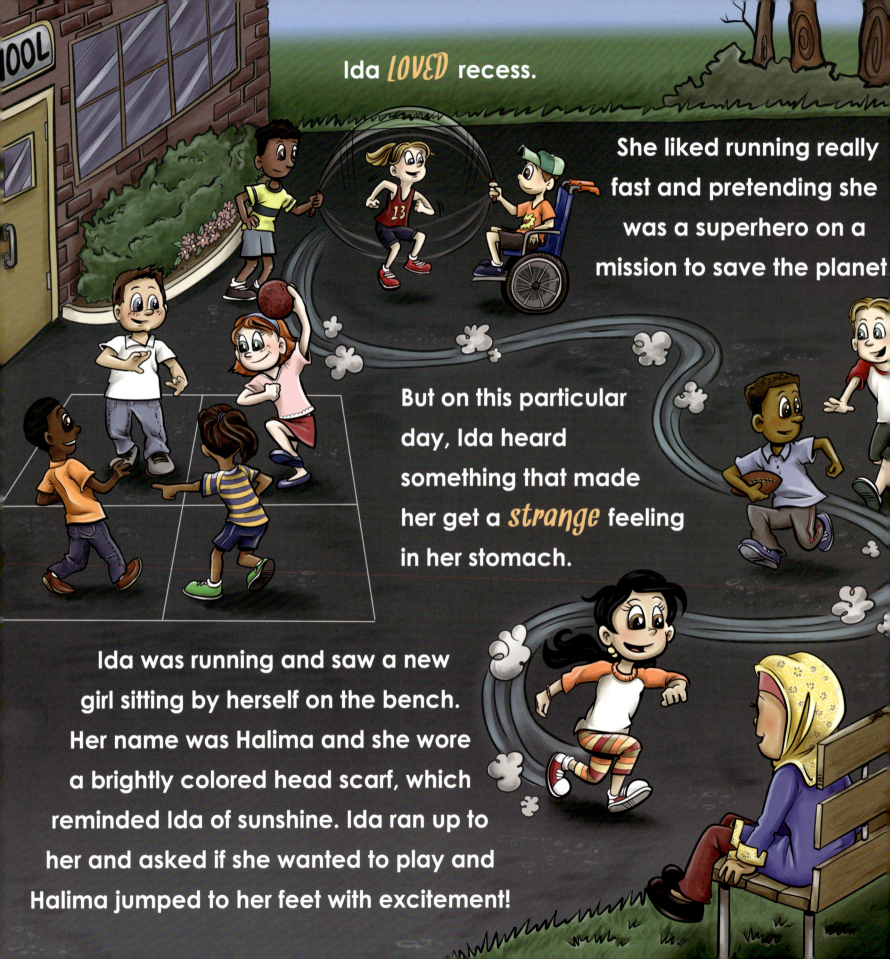

Just then, another girl ran up to Ida and whispered that she shouldn't play with Halima. Ida didn't understand. The girl said that her parents told her that she wasn't allowed to play with Halima because she was Muslim, so she wasn't a nice person. Ida thought, "**Ouch!** Doesn't she know that everyone wants a friend?"

Ida felt confused because Halima seemed really kind. Ida didn't know what to say and no longer felt like playing, so she slowly walked away.

Ida thought of Smalls and the words she had started to hear...

I know WHO will bring the hero out in YOU.

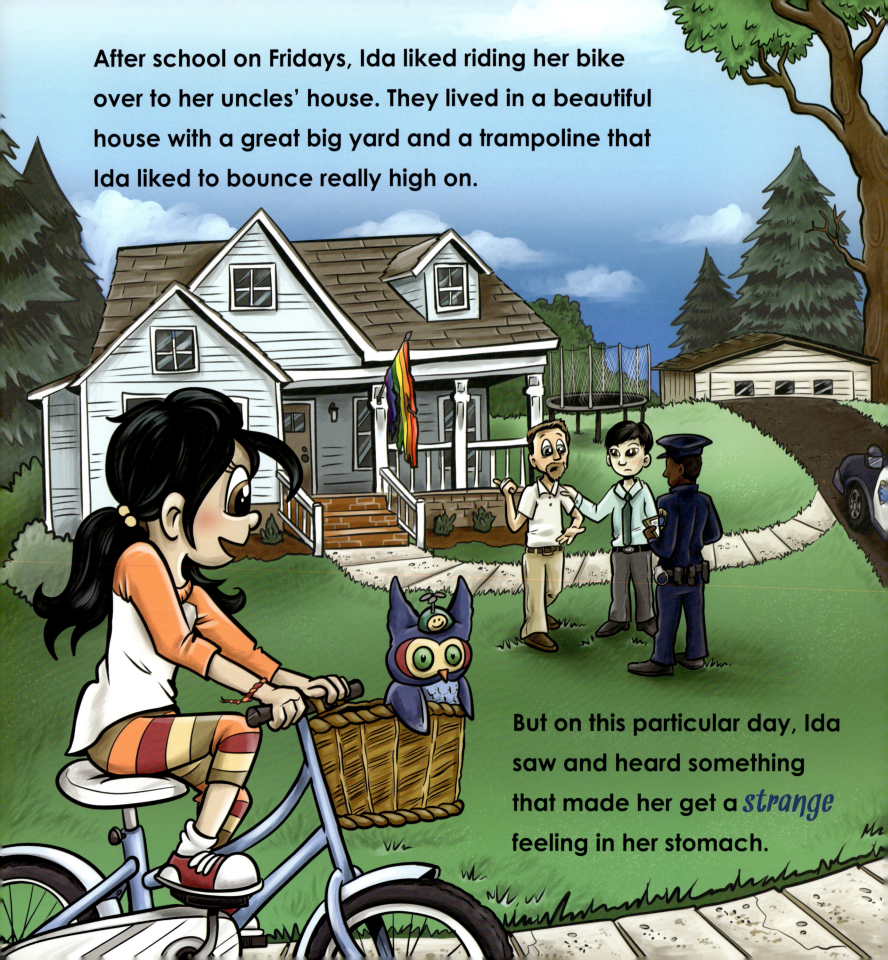

After school on Fridays, Ida liked riding her bike over to her uncles' house. They lived in a beautiful house with a great big yard and a trampoline that Ida liked to bounce really high on.

But on this particular day, Ida saw and heard something that made her get a *strange* feeling in her stomach.

As she made her way up their driveway, Ida saw her uncles talking to a police officer and pointing to their torn rainbow flag. Ida jumped off her bike and grabbed Smalls. She ran up to her uncles, gave them both a big hug and asked what had happened.

Uncle Jun said there were people who thought the love between them was wrong. Ida became sad and mad all at the same time.

She hugged Smalls and thought, "Don't people know everybody is loveable?" Then she heard Smalls whisper ... "I know *WHO* will bring the hero out in *YOU*."

After hearing what had happened the day before, Ida's parents took her to the park to cheer her up.

They always liked going to the park for picnics, playing ball, and having ice cream. But on this particular day, Ida experienced something that made her get a *strange* feeling in her stomach.

Ida and her parents were playing a three-person baseball game where Ida's mom was the pitcher, her dad was the batter, and Ida was the outfielder because she was a really good catcher.

Ida's mom threw a perfect pitch, and dad hit it high and long. Ida started running after it when her dad saw her running toward the street.

Ida's dad ran fast to save her from a car when someone yelled, "Stop him, he's trying to grab that little girl!"

When dad had Ida safely in his arms, he turned and said, "She's my daughter!" Some people didn't believe him.

When Ida's mom reached them she said, "That's my husband and this is *our* child!"

One person looked at the three of them with hate, another with embarrassment and one asked if everyone was OK.

At first Ida felt confused but then she looked into her parents' eyes and felt pride. In that moment, she knew she was the perfect combination of her mom and dad.

She thought of Smalls and the words she heard getting louder. "I know *WHO* will bring the hero out in *YOU*."

Exhausted by what had just happened,
Ida and her parents quietly gathered up their picnic and got
into the car. Ida hugged Smalls and found the courage to tell
about her week and how it made her feel.

She explained how Dev was made fun of because he wore braces.

Ida said she felt icky when Tommy sat too close and hugged her.

Ida told them how she wanted to play with the new girl but was told not to, and that she was upset about her uncles' flag.

Then today, people said mean things about her family. She asked, "Why does my stomach feel *strange* every time someone says or does something mean? Why can't I find the right words?"

Back at home, Ida's parents explained when people say and do mean things, it's often out of fear, lack of understanding, or intolerance. **Intolerance** is when a person doesn't accept another person for who they are, what they look like, where they come from, their faith, or culture.

Ida's parents told her that *strange* feeling in her stomach meant she was listening to her gut ~ her inside voice of what's right and wrong. Her parents told her to always listen to her gut.

That's when Ida realized she was *extraordinary* because she listened to her gut. Now, she had the power to stand up and speak out when someone was being treated unfairly.

Ida's parents said they knew just the place where they could go and be with other people who had found their voices. Ida's heart grew bigger. She felt happy inside and hugged her parents tightly. She said:

I know who will bring the hero out in me....

Ida B. Wells Barnett

The main character of this book got her name from Ida Bell Wells (July 16, 1862 to March 25, 1931), better known as Ida B. Wells. Ida was an African-American journalist, newspaper publisher, abolitionist, and feminist who led an anti-lynching crusade in the United States in the 1890s. Ida stood up to discrimination and advocated for the rights of people. She went on to found and be an integral member of many groups striving for voting rights and social justice.

Ida's sidekick owl named Smalls got its name from Robert Smalls. He was an American hero, businessman, and publisher. He also served in the House of Representatives from South Carolina. We encourage you to visit your local library for more information about them and other heroes that stood up and spoke out for love and tolerance.

To continue in Ida's legacy of advocacy, a portion of the proceeds from the sales of these books will be donated to organizations that address issues of inequity.

THANK YOU

to all of our supporters, who helped us bring Ida to life!

Rajan & Amar
Rick & Carol McGowan
Nichole Bethel
Kevin Mccloskey
The Horvat Family
Ellie Pugh
Elysia J. Mancini Duerr Esq.
Dr. Kathleen Briseno
Mary Beth Condara
John Shepherd
Chandra Connor
Tracy Gius
Dorothy Illson
David Somogyi
Meg Lancaster
Ellen Weiner
Dagmar McGannon
Scott Ricketts
Cheryl Jankowski
Jim Foley
Dwayne Farver
James Stever
Nan Hayley-Delzani
Barry & Anna Cohen

C. Smith
Barbara V. Ciricillo
Sharon Pennock
Amy Leary & Laurent Bibonne
Mirrah Fisher
Becks Antoszewski
Uncle Billy
Mark, Tina, Dylan & Oliver Quinto
Meg Clark
in honor of Alexander Anthony Rubbo
Judi Clover-Flick
Laurie & Vince Cardinale
Andrew M Anderson II
Bonnie Devine
Pamela Geick
Michael Sanson
Redman
Colleen Foley
Delaney Foley
Brian Bucher
Pattie & Mark Frentzel
John Terry
Patrick Foley
Dick Clough

Kristen Larson
Jonathon & Maura
Damon & Aileen
Bill Williams
Deb Smith
Dennis & Martha Griffin
El Joneso
The Kerber Family
Grammy Sue
Mike & Debbie Casey
Ian Schwarber
Lee & Susan Cassanelli
Dina Smith
Karen Webb
H-CAN *(Havertown Community Action Network)*

Meet the Ida Team

Author

Dr. Kate Anderson Foley's personal and professional life has been grounded in social justice and for breaking down the barriers for children who historically have been marginalized. She believes that all children, regardless of background and circumstance, deserve the very best that education has to offer and that it is up to the collective "we" to make that happen.
You can learn more about Kate at www.edpolicyconsulting.com

Author

Jenifer Anderson-Smith Jenifer Anderson-Smith has committed her life to activism and community service. Inspired by her father's creation of a community-wide dialogue initiative and by her own lived experience of raising four biracial children, Jenifer holds the cause of sparking honest and constructive dialogue about race close to her heart. She has worked for years as a basketball coach and official as well as with underprivileged teens. In recent years, she has jumped into grassroots community work to promote racial justice and other social causes. Jenifer is active in local politics and various civic organizations. She is a lover of music, diversity and laughter, all things her family provides.

Illustrator

Dawn Griffin is a designer/illustrator/cartoonist living in Havertown PA, specializing in kids and young adult material. Her creator-owned properties include the sci-fi/humor comic "Zorphbert & Fred", and the self-esteem kids book series "Abby's Adventures" published under Eifrig Publishing. She has also contributed to multiple anthologies such as "Team Cul de Sac" from Andrews McMeel Publishing, and "RISE: Comics Against Bullying" from Northwest Press. "Creative Workhorse" may be an understatement. You can view her portfolio at www.dawnrgriffinstudios.com